Contents

THE ROLE PLAYED BY BODOLAND TERRITORIAL COUNCIL OF ASSAM IN DEVELOPING A FRIENDLY RELATION BETWEEN INDIA AND BHUTAN

RITURAJ BASUMATARY | SWMAOSHAR BRAHMA

Abbreviation

BTC -Bodoloand Territorial Council

BTR - Bodoland Territorial Region

SAARC - South Asian Association for Regional Cooperation

ASEAN -Associationof Southeast Asian Nation

BTAD – Bodoland Territorial Area District

UNO – United Nation Organization

HEPs - Hydroelectric Projects

UGC - University Grants Commission

PSUs – Public Sector Undertakings

ICCR – Indian Council for Cultural Exchange

DAHE – Department of Adult and Higher Education

RGoB – Royal Government of Bhutan

ITEC – Indian Technical and Economic Program

TCS –Tata Consultancy Service

ISRO – Indian Space Research Organization

CPWD - Central Public Works Department

ITES – Information Technology Enabled Service

RBA – Royal Bhutan Army

RBG – Royal Bodyguard of Bhutan

NDA - National Defence Academy

IMA – Indian Military Academy

SSB – Shastra Seema Bal

BIMSTEC – Bay of Bengal Initiative for Multi-Sectoral Technical and Economic Cooperation

NESRIP - North Eastern States Road Investment Project

BAC – Bodoland Autonomous Council

BLT – Bodo Liberation Tigers

MLA – Member of Legislative Assembly

PWD – Public Works Department

MCLA - Member of Bodoland Territorial Council

BCCI - Bhutan Chambers of Commerce and Industry

NDFB – National Democratic Front of Bodoland

BRAWFED - Bodoland Regional Apex Weavers & Artisans Cooperative Federation Ltd

TEIH – Thematic Exhibition on Indian Handicrafts

SAI – Sports Authority of India

KLO – Kamatapur Liberation Organization

ULFA – United Liberation Front of Assam

ATTF- All Tripura Tiger Force

NSCN - National Socialist Council of Nagaland

BLTF - Bodo Liberation Tigers Force

BIFA - Bhutan-India Friendship Association

CHAPTER I

INTRODUCTION

The bilateral ties between Bhutan and India have always been close and both nations share a "special friendship" and have been through the test of times. India, to date, remains influential over Bhutan's foreign policy, defence and commerce. The Himalayan Kingdom of Bhutan and Republic of India has been traditionally close and both countries share special relationship making Bhutan a protected state but not protectorate of India. Beside, several plans and policies of the Indian government for the strong relationship, the steps taken by the Bodoloand Territorial Council government along with Assam government is unforgettable.

Bodoland Territorial Region is an autonomous region in the state of Assam in India and it is a Bodo community dominated area comprising four districts Kokrajhar, Chirang, Udalguri and Baksa on the north bank of the Brahmaputra River, by the foothills of Bhutan and Arunachal Pradesh. Behind the developing relationship between the India and Bhutan in every field like Economy, Political, Cultural Exchange and Such a close contact with people to people in a border area, the role play by people of Bodoland Territorial Region and its government is very important to discuss.

The location of the Bodoland Territorial Region is quite advantage for people of both the countries that they can any time cross the border with taking official permission and carry out trading activities. If we go to this borderarea wecan see lots of people in this border area getting advantage by opening small scale business and running their family. Under, the Chirang District there isSamtaibari road which go directly through to the Bhutan Entrance gate which is known as Gelephu. Through, this road several travelers from both the countries make up's and down. It helps the local people to grow up in more business related activities.

OBJECTIVES

- To understand the developing relationship between India and Bhutan.
- To know the steps taken by Bodoland Territorial Council government and People of this region.
- To understand the economy and livelihood advantages of both the countries in bordering area.

HYPOTHESIS

- The developing relationship between two countries playing a counter role for the China.
- The relationship revives the India's "Neighborhood First" policy.

METHODOLOGY AND DATA COLLECTION

The study took various methodologies to collect the data from various sources. The methodology is adopted according to the need and objective of the study. The present study is using both the primary and secondary method of data collection. The data collected from various books along with observation and Telephonic conversation with friends from border areas between India and Bhutan. The topic is studied through secondary sources like internet, magazines, journals, books, articles, newspapers and so on.

REVIEW OF RELATED LITERATURE

The Present study is sought to undergo reviewing some available literature, which however might not solely relevant for the proposed area of research. However, it may provide the valuable grounds to understand and help in examining the steps taken by the Bodoland Territorial Council government and its people in carrying out a fruitful relationship between India and Bhutan. Therefore, attempts are being made for basic conceptual, theoretical and problem understanding the Indo-Bhutan relationship and different views examined by different thinkers and authors.

Satish Kumar in his book "India-China Major Disputes Nepal, Bhutan and Tibet" discuss about after the Narendra came in to power in 2014 and giving more importance to Himalayan state like Bhutan, Nepal and Tibet in order to make development in strategically as well as India's defence in this region. Over all from the book we can understand that as anIndia'sNeighborhood first policy the relationship must be strengthen in order to make development both in diplomacy and factors related to the defence.

Madhu Rajput in the book "Indo Bhutan Relation through Prism of History" stated Bhutan as closest relation with India. The book attempt to evaluate the relationship between two countries starting from the 20th century along with role played by India in strengthening and emergence of Bhutan from isolation to International Arena.

Arif Hussien Malik and Nazir Ahmed Sheikh in his articles " Changing Dynamic of Indo-Bhutan Relations: Implications for India" studied about the importance of neighbor countries in determining foreign policy and advantage of creating good relationship in order to make overall development in Political and Economy field. They, view Bhutan as the main weapons of India countering against China as well as highlighting the result of Unfriendly relation between China and Pakistan.

Asha Basumatary in her articles "Bodo-Bhutia Border Trade Relation in Colonial Era" giving us fruitful information about the colonial era as how the people of bordering area exchange certain commodities and improve economic living style. She tried to explore the brotherhood and sisterhood relationship of how Bodo tribes carried out border trade with Bhutia tribes of Bhutan during colonial times and also to examine how far it contributed to the growth of economy. I believe that there have been so many changes in the trading characteristics between two countries so it's importance to study the present structure of trading and how itcontributes to development both countries economically and politically.

From , News paper Economic Times Sep 12/2018, Border trade centre between India and Bhutan inaugurated at Darranga in Tamulpur, Baksa district, which is also located in Bodoland Territorial region. The steps were taken by the Assam government along with the BTC government and stated also construction of 264 km of border roads for the development of Bodoland district. If we imagine about all this plans and policies of both Assam and BTC government the relationship is swiping in a better way compares to earlier of 20th century.

Sailen Debnath in his book "Indo-Bhutan Relation in Modern Times" wrote about multidimensional aspect of relation between India and Bhutan and considered the best relationship between big and small country. He highlighted issues of strategic, communicational, cultural and security related independence and India's overall India's contribution to the Bhutan economic and infrastructural development. He give us complete understanding about the role some North East base insurgency group which are taking shelter in Bhutan. Overall, we can say that the book giving us complete details about several factors playing important role in building permanent relationship between two countries.

Niharika Tiwari in her book "Preferential Trade Agreement in South Asia and SAARC" discussing about two main aspect of relation as Economic and Regionalism and how these two play a big role in creating a relationships between countries. Here, she was trying to understand the role of some organization like SAARC,

ASEAN in the development of friendly and co-operation between countries along with the factor of Preferential Trade Agreements in the bilateral trade among countries. From, this book we can get a knowledge about the geographical location of the country and the level of economic development by which it affect in determining countries foreign policy .

From, the article "India Together" Bodo weavers spin money in Bhutan stated about the emergence of Bodo women weaving as livelihood option. The article gives us details knowledge about the increasing social entrepreneurship activities of Bodo community and in relation to this those products found a good market in the Bhutan. This, kind of exchange of products and market excess between the countries make relationship and foreign policy tighter.

Dr. Keshab Basumatary, in his book "A Short Profile of Human Development in Bodoland Territorial Area District of Assam" discuss about socio- economic development of Bodo community. He focuses a deeper look on the issue through the new development paradigm. Identity, as recognized by the proponents of new development paradigm, plays a crucial role in human life. Dr Basumatary applies clear theoretical sense of development economics in his present assessment and the write up will bring a total picture of profile of progress of an ethnic group living in Assam. From, this book we can understand that the development of Bodo community is lacking and in order to change this we have to take active step individually and increase the role social entrepreneurship. With, reference to the Bodo people living in bordering area and development in livelihood activities is noticeable.

RELEVANCE OF STUDY

In modern times no state can avoid involvement in the international sphere. This involvement must be systematic and based on some well defined principles. The principle and the purpose of a state is reflected in foreign policy. The importance of foreign policy is accepted widely and it basically defines a state's approach towards the other state. A foreign policy should protect the territorial integrity of the country and protect the interest of its citizen, both within and outside the country. The objective of foreign policy should be the maintenance of links with other members of international community and adoption of policy of conflict or co-operation towards them with a view to promote it'd own interest. Moreover, the foreign policy of country should seek to promote and further it's national interest of the country. The primary interest of each state is preservation, security and well being of its citizen. Often, the interest of various state come in clash and the state has their interest bearing in mind this factor.

In this regard the study is on the Far East side from the main land India with view to understand new topic and new environment of Bodoland Territorial Region of Assam in Development a relationship between Bhutan. This study will give us a theoretical and practicalknowledge about the peace and conflict relationship between the people of both the countries with special reference to the community living in the bordering area.

PLAN OF WORK

The work is planned under the four chapters.

The chapter 1 will have its introductory part, which basically deals with introduction about the study along with Objectives, Review of literature, Methodology and Relevance of study.

The chapter 2 will focus upon a short profile on the past and present diplomatic and foreign policy relation between two countries. Study, on the agreement and plans-policies on economic, political and geographical background. The steps taken Central Government outside the role of BTC administration and Assam Government.

The chapter 3 will comes to main agenda of the study, action taken by Bodoland Territorial Council government with relation to the Assam government along with communities in the field of Economy, Trade, Social-CulturalPrograms, Infrastructure, of this region in developing a relation. Here, the writing is on the overall development activities taken by both Assam governments in relation to the BTC government.

The, 4 concluding part will be deal with Summary of the findings, Recommendation and Bibliography.

CHAPTER II

THE PAST AND PRESENT RELATIONSHIP; INDIA-BHUTAN

A tiny landlocked state located in the Eastern Himalayas, Bhutan has historically shared deep religious-cultural links with India. India-Bhutan relationship is relatively closest compares to other South Asian Association for Regional Cooperation countries. There has been like a big brother relationship between India-Bhutan since time immoral. According to, time and environment the relationship has been like a sea wave direction. The relationship starts from the 699 km long attaching both the countries and adjoins the Indian states of Assam (267 km), Arunachal Pradesh(217 km), West Bengal(183 km) and Sikkim(32 km). Guru Padmasambhava, a Buddhist saint who went to Bhutan from India had played an influential role in spreading Buddhism and strengthening traditional ties in both the nations.

Beginning Phase

Starting from 20th century India played a vital role in helping hand development with Bhutan. For, much of its history, Bhutan preserved its isolation from the outside world, staying out of international organization and maintaining few bilateral relation. Government of India has consistently supporting the socio economic development of Bhutan starting from Military to Hydropower project. Bhutan was a protectorate of British India and came under the British suzerainty in 1865. "The treaty of Punakha" was signed with British in 1910 for the future development of both countries and become a protectorate of British India after a signing a treaty in 1910 allowing the British to "guide"its foreign and affairs and defence. Bhutan was one of the first to recognize India's independence in 1947 and both nations fostered close relation, their importance augmented by the annexation of Tibet in 1950 by the People's Republic of China and It's border disputes with both Bhutan and India, which close ties with Nepal and Bhutan to be central to its "Himalayan frontiers". Since, then relationship between the countries has become stronger.

The diplomatic relation between two countries started with the signing of "Treaty of Friendship and Co-operation" in 1949, calling for peace between two nations and non-interference in each other's internal affairs. The treaty also established free trade and extradition protocols. The occupation of Tibet by Communist China brought both nations ever more closely as Bhutan also the feelings internal affairs and control by the Communist China. In 1958, the then Prime Minister Jawaharlal Nehru visited Bhutan and reiterated India's support for Bhutan's independence and later declared in the Indian Parliament that any aggression against Bhutan would seen as aggression against India. The relationship has been sustained by a tradition of regular high level visits and dialogues between the two countries. In August 1959, there was a rumor in India political circle that China was seeking to 'liberate' Sikkim and Bhutan. Nehru stated in the Lok Sabha that the defence of the territorial uprightness and frontiers of Bhutan was the responsibility of the Government of India. This statement was immediately objected by Prime Minister of Bhutan, saying Bhutan is not a protectorate of India nor did the treaty involve national defence of any sort.The feelings of small geographical background and level of development is a big issue for the Bhutan. In its relation with India, since the late 1950s, Bhutan has repeatedly made efforts to assert its independent identity and had to reduce its dependence of India as the feelings of over dependence will lead to affect in the Bhutan's internal affairs. During the Sino-Indian war of 1962, the Bhutanese king declined to offer a base to the Indian troops.In 1968, Bhutan reciprocated in 1971. The two offices of special representative were upgraded to fully fledged embassies in1978.Special office of India was established in Bhutan.Bhutan had obtained the UN membership in 1971 and elevated its diplomatic status in New Delhi to full ambassadorial level and established diplomatic relations with nations independent of India's opinions.

The period saw a major increase in India's economic, military and development aid to Bhutan, which had also embarked on a programme of modernization to bolster its security. While India repeatedly reiterated its military support to Bhutan, the latter expressed concerns about India's ability to protect Bhutan against China while fighting a two-front war involving Pakistan. The relation with the Communist China was a big boost for both countries in making suitable and developmental relationship. The time and environment frequently make them to stay together and counter the relationship with China. Despite good relations, India and Bhutan did not complete a detailed demarcation of their borders until the period between 1973 and 1984. Border demarcation talks with India generally resolved disagreements except for several small sectors, including the middle zone between Sarpang and Geylegphug and the eastern frontier with the Indian state of Arunachal Pradesh.

Areas of Co-operation

Trade

India is Bhutan's largest trading partner. The India-Bhutan Trade and Transit agreement 1972 established a free trade regime between the two countries. The first agreement on Trade and Commerce between India and Bhutan was signed in 1972. Since then, the agreement has been renewed five times.There are a number of Institutional mechanisms between India and Bhutan in areas such as security, border management, trade and transit, economic, hydropower, water resources. There have been regular exchanges at the Ministerial and Official's level exchanges of Parliamentarian delegation to strengthen partnership in diverse areas of co-operation. The export and imports product mostly include electricity, light oils, Motor spirit (gasoline) including aviation spirit (petrol), Ferrous products obtained by direct reduction of iron ore, Portland cement, Dolomite, Carbides of calcium, Carbides of silicon, Cement clinkers, timber and wood product, Potatoes, Cardamom and fruit product's. Bilateral Trade is conducted in Indian Rupees which is fully convertible to Ngultrum at par. Though, Bhutan has an adverse balance of trade with India.

According to Eleventh Five Year Plan(2013-2018) of Bhutan has a total budget outlay of Ngultrum21300 crore, with self reliance and inclusive green socio-economic development as the key objectives. Government of India committed to support Bhutan's 11th Five Year Plan with economic assistance of Rupees 4500 crore. The Government of India reiterated its commitment to Bhutan's socio-economic development and assured full support Bhutan's 12th Five Year Plan (2018-2023).

Hydropower

India is playing an important role in development of hydropower projects. This not only provides Bhutanese with electricity for domestic use but also revenue from surplus electricity exported to India. Hydropower projects in Bhutan are an example of win-win cooperation, providing a reliable source of inexpensive and clean electricity to India, generating export revenue for Bhutan and cementing our economic integration. India-Bhutan hydropower cooperation began in 1961 with the signing of the Jaldhaka agreement. The Jaldhaka project is situated on the Indian side of Indo-Bhutan border of West Bengal. The major part of power produced at Jaldhaka hydropower plant was exported to southern Bhutan. So far, Government of India has constructed three Hydroelectric Projects (HEPs) in Bhutan totaling 1416 MW (336 MW Chukha HEP, 60 MW Kurichhu HEP and 1020 MW Tala HEP), which are operational and exporting surplus power to India About three-fourth of the power generated is exported and rest is used for domestic consumption. Some power sharing agreements are mention below

- The agreement on Cooperation in the field of Hydroelectric Power (HEP) in July 2006, which outlines the framework for cooperation in the field of Hydropower.

- In May 2008, the two sides have signed the Protocol to the 2006 agreement.
- In 2014, the two countries have also signed the "Framework Inter-Governmental Agreement" concerning the development of Joint Venture Hydropower projects through PSUs of the same.

Under the Protocol of 2006 agreement, Government of India has agreed to assist Royal Government of Bhutan in developing a minimum of 10,000 MW of hydropower and import the surplus electricity from this to India by the year 2020. Currently, there are three Inter-Governmental (IG) model HEPs viz. 1200 MW Punatsangchhu-I, 1020 MW Punatsangchhu-II and 720 MW Mangdechhu under implementation. In April 2014, an Inter-Governmental Agreement was signed between India and Bhutan for development of four more HEP's of capacity 2120 MW (600 MW Kholongchhu, 180 MW Bunakha, 570 MW Wangchhu and 770 MW Chamkharchhu) under the Joint Venture Model. These projects will have both the JV partners owning 50:50 shareholdings each in the JV-Company. Debt-equity ratio would be 70:30, with equity shared equally between JV partners. Further, MEA is providing Druk Green Power Corporation's (Bhutanese) share of equity as grant.

India's support in the development of the hydropower sector in Bhutan is the centerpiece of Bhutan-India economic cooperation and is one of the main pillars of bilateral cooperation. The cooperation in the hydropower sector is full of opportunities and has been recognized by both Bhutan and India as being mutually beneficial. India finds her interests fulfilled in alleviating their power deficiency by supporting Bhutan and Bhutan in turn finds an opportunity to optimize its national income through power exports to India. This sustainable win-win situation for both sides makes the relationship between the two nations even stronger and long lasting.

Educational Cooperation

Popularity of India as an education destination for Bhutanese students is a reference- point for close bilateral ties. Today, as many as one third of Bhutan's student population are pursuing higher education in India. The education sector reflects the friendly relation Bhutan and India. Bhutan's indigenous higher education institution, a fairly recent phenomenon in Bhutan, India has over the years played a major role in human resource development in Bhutan.

Role of Higher education has been the key to cooperation between the two countries, as identified by Indian President Pranab Mukherjee during his visit to the country last year. Nearly, 5000 Bhutanese students study in India today and 800 of these are benefitting from scholarships. It's no denying that several higher educational institutes in India run or function in a way that contradicts the University Grants Commission (UGC) directives or even educational laws. The UGC websites runs alerts with names of such unrecognized universities and colleges in India. However, education is on concurrent list in India and hence laws of federal states also give recognition to colleges and universities. Bhutan must incorporate such alerts provided by Indian agencies like the UGC with a dedicated portal for disseminating them to students. The educational fairs that Bhutan allows universities and colleges to hold in which India features regularly must also be examined for the claims the colleges make. Some important scholarships for those Bhutanese students who study inIndian institution are;

- Under Graduate and Post –Graduate Scholarships Government of India scholarships are granted to Bhutanese students at Undergraduate level every year to study in prestigious Indian Institutions of higher learning. Under this scheme, 450 slots have been approved for Bhutanese students to pursue Under Graduate courses in India.
- Nehru-Wang chuck Scholarships Prestigious Nehru-Wangchuk Scholarship is being awarded to deserving and talented Bhutanese nationals to undertake studies in selected and premier Indian educational Institutions.
- Ambassador's Scholarship Ambassador's scholarship is being awarded to meritorious and deserving Bhutanese students who are studying in various/colleges in India on self financing basis as well as to other suitable candidates.
- Aid-to-Bhutan Indian Council of Cultural Research Scholarship twenty fully funded slots are provided

every year to Bhutanese students under Indian Council of Cultural Research Scholarship. The Aid-to Bhutan Indian Council of Cultural Research Scholarship scheme has been implemented in Bhutan from the academic session 2012-13. Students selected under this scheme are placed in the prestigious engineering colleges in India. The Scholarship is awarded by Government of India on the advice of Department of Adult and Higher Education (DAHE), Ministry of Education, Royal Government of Bhutan, based on the merit ranking of the student in Class XII. Since its inception in 2012, ninety-six (96) students have availed of this scholarship. For the academic year 2017-18, twenty students were selected under this scholarship scheme and seventeen out of them have been placed in prestigious Indian Engineering Colleges.

- ITEC Training Programme Scheme Every year GoI provides 300 training slots under ITEC programme and a further 60 slots under Tata Consultancy Service Colombo Plan in various fields to Bhutanese for upgrading their administrative and technical skills. Under this scheme trainees are provided with airfare, tuition fee accommodation and living allowance by GoI. 40 additional slots were granted last year to this Mission during the mid-term review and Mission had availed of 282 slots under this Scheme. Besides these regular slots, many special courses are also being conducted in various Indian institutions for Bhutanese candidates.

Cooperation between India and Bhutan is set to intensify and also in the education sector in the years to come and the number of students studying in India is in the future going to continue being one third of the total student population of the country. Bhutanese students enjoy the friendly atmosphere that they find in India. New Delhi and federal states of India along with the Thimphu must take measures to increase transparency,accountability and efficiency in regulating admission and study of Bhutanese students in India.

Technology Cooperation

Bhutan seeks to develop its digital and space sectors to fulfill the aspiration of its new generation and India has stepped up to facilitate this endeavor. In the 51st year of diplomatic relations, India and Bhutan added a new chapter to their bilateral cooperation by expanding their engagement to digital and space domains. Several key initiatives were launched by the prime ministers of India and Bhutan in the digital and space sectors on 17 August 2019, such as RuPay, integration of DrukREN with National Knowledge Network of India and inauguration of the Ground Earth Station constructed by Indian Space Research Organization. Bhutan being a landlocked country with limited internal and external connectivity has had issues accessing the world market. To overcome this handicap and be connected to the world through the digital domain, it has embarked on a journey to develop its digital sector. Bhutan seeks to reduce its over dependence on the hydropower sector for exports, revenue generation and employment generation due to its lack of sustainability in the long run. Redirecting focus towards the digital sector is thus, a more reliable source for employment generation and foreign exchange earnings through exports of IT and IT Enabled Services (ITES). Keeping this in mind, the first tech park and incubation center was established in Thimphu in 2012 to attract foreign investments and generate jobs for the youth. The new government under PM Lotay Tshering is also, focusing on developing Bhutan's digital and space infrastructure to harness the potential of the youth through adequate generation of employment while ensuring that skill development remains at par with world standards. In 2016, the Government of India approved signing of a Memorandum of Understanding with Bhutan on technical cooperation in the field of capacity building, benchmarking and bilateral exchange in infrastructure engineering. The MoU aims at taking forward India-Bhutan friendship treaty and provide an umbrella for educational, scientific and technical research and environment protection. Through this Memorandum of Understanding (MoU), the Central Public Works Department (CPWD), a construction major under the Urban Development Ministry, will gain experience in construction of roads on hills which will be helpful in Jammu and Kashmir, Himachal Pradesh, Uttarakhand and various States of North-East Region.India and Bhutan have begun their digital cooperation through initiatives that cater to the banking and education sectors. The collaboration in the space domain mainly pertains to harnessing the services of the South Asia Satellite. One of the defining collaborations has been in the banking sector, with the launch of RuPay. Repay's rollout revolutionizes financial transactions and paves the way for financial inclusion in Bhutan, which faces difficulties in providing physical infrastructure such as banks and ATMs to its remote areas. The benefit accruing to India is mainly an increase in the global reach of its indigenous payment system and increase in digital payments across the two countries thus easing tourism and cross border business transactions. To promote cashless transactions within Bhutan, an agreement on studying the feasibility of launching India's BHIM app was also signed. The focus of India-Bhutan relations in the digital age has turned towards the youth while maintaining the traditional aspects of the relations. Bhutan seeks to develop its digital and space sectors to fulfill the aspirations of its new generation and India has stepped up to facilitate this endeavor that the mountain kingdom intends to take forward.

Military and Border Cooperation

With intense support from India, the Royal Bhutan Army was formed in the 1950s in response to the Chinese takeover and subsequent People's Liberation Army actions in Tibet. In 1958, the royal government introduced a conscription system and plans for a standing army of 2,500 soldiers. The Indian government had also repeatedly urged and pressured Bhutan to end its neutrality or isolationist policy and accept Indian economic and military assistance. This was because India considered Bhutan one of the most vulnerable sectors in its strategic defense system in regards to China. Indian Military Training Team is permanently based in western Bhutan to train the Royal Bhutan Army, while other units cooperate with the Royal Bhutan Army. The Indian Army maintains a training mission in Bhutan, known as the Indian Military Training Team, which is responsible for the training of Royal Bhutan Army and Royal Bodyguard of Bhutan personnel. All Royal Bhutan Army and Royal Bodyguard of Bhutan officers are trained at the Indian Army's officer training institutes, namely the National Defence Academy (NDA) in Pune, and the Indian Military Academy (IMA) in Dehradun.Project DANTAK of the Border Roads Organization, a subdivision of the Indian Army Corps of Engineers, has been operating in Bhutan since May 1961. Since then Project DANTAK has been responsible for the construction and maintenance of over 1,500 km of roads and bridges, Paro Airport and Yongphulla Airport (upgraded in 2018, with scheduled fixed-wing civilian flights), heliports and other infrastructure. While these serve India's strategic defense needs as well as obvious economic benefit for the people of Bhutan.

The Bhutan- India border is the international border separating Bhutan and India. The Border is 699 Km long. The border between Bhutan and India is the only land access to make ups and down. The entry point is the Jaigaon in the Indian state of West Bengal and Gelephu side of Chirang District, Assam. The Indian government deploys 12 battalions of Sashtra Seema Bal and there are

132 border posts, to guard the border on its side. The bilateral Indian-Bhutan Group Border Management and Security has been established to collaboratively assess and secure the border between the two countries. There exists a secretary level mechanism to deal with the management of border and security related matters between the two nations. There is also the Border District Coordination Meeting mechanism between the bordering states and the Royal Government of Bhutan to facilitate coordination on border management and other related matters.In 2011, 7th India-Bhutan meeting on Border Management and Security was held at New Delhi. The Indian delegation was led by A.E. Ahmad; Secretary (Border Management), Ministry of Home Affairs and the Bhutanese delegation was led by Dasho Penden Wangchuk, Secretary, Ministry of Home and Cultural Affairs (MHCA).
The two sides reviewed issues relating to threat perceptions, security and border management issues, sharing of real time information, SSB escorts, opening of a seasonal Land Customs Station at Jiti, training of security personnel, misuse of SIM Cards, coordination of entry-exit points on the Indo-Bhutan border, etc.

Border management is a security function that calls for coordination and concerted action by various government agencies within our country. The aim is to secure our frontiers and safeguard our nation from the risks involved in the movement of goods and people from India to other countries and vice versa. Effective border management is must for both the country because it strengthens the security related matters and safeguards the country from

other illegal or violation of rules activities.

Importance of Bhutan

The importance of Bhutan for India spreads over in the field of Geographical, Economic and Political etc. Bhutan is central to India's foreign policies as the member of such organization like SAARC, BIMSTEC as well as policies like Act east policy and Neighborhoods first policy. Marked by a history of political divisions, economic differences, and geostrategic divergences, the Indian subcontinent remains deeply divided, with exceptionally low levels of integration. No other regional power is as disconnected from its immediate neighborhood as India. Recognizing this disconnect as a challenge to India's economic and security interests, Prime Minister Narendra Modi playing a important intra- and inter-regional connectivity a policy priority since 2014. Special emphasis is given by India on the Neighborhood first Policy and its relationship with Bhutan, which is mostly tension free. Narendra Modi said that India-Bhutan partnership forms an important pillar of Indian government's 'Neighborhood First' policy and expressed confidence that his two-day trip beginning Saturday will promote the time-tested ties between the two countries. Narendra Modi stated "India-Bhutan partnership is a special character and substance and forms an important pillar of Government of India's 'Neighborhood First' policy. Some of the important point that we can mention are below-

- Bhutan shares border with four Indian States: Assam, Arunachal Pradesh, West Bengal and Sikkim. It helps people for business and Tourism purposes.
- Nestled in the Himalayas, Bhutan serves as a buffer between India and China. Bhutan play as a security weapons for India.
- Bhutan's strategic location has helped India to flush out militant groups in the North East India.
- Since 1990s, Bhutan has repeatedly turned down China's "Package deal" that offers a bigger territorial concession to Bhutan in return for the smaller Doklam area.
- Bhutan role in the Doklam standoff between India and China shows its dogmatic stance and the ability to assert the status quo in the face of Chinese intrusions.
- Bordering area has been very active for organizing cultural activities and linguistic cooperation by which there will be brotherhood relation.

- Bhutan provides a market for Indian commodities and is a destination for Indian investment.

- A politically stable Bhutan is important to India. An unstable and restive Bhutan can provide a safe haven to anti-India activities and anti-India militant group.

Therefore, importance of Bhutan for India is significant and India must co-operate every problem that Bhutan has faced today either economy or socio cultural. For the further development and peaceful cooperation there must be a time to time meetings and conference, which will

make relationship stronger.

Present relation under Narendra Modi's Government

After the Narendra Modi led BJP coalition government came in to power in 2014 by Wining General Election the relationship between two countries got new meaning. He visited Bhutan as the first foreign destination, as the step of neighborhood first policy. He had inaugurated the Supreme Court complex in Bhutan and also promised help to to Bhutan on IT and digital sector.Modi made his first foreign visit to Bhutan after an invitation by Bhutan King Jigme Khesar Namgyel Wang chuck and Tobgay. The visit was name by the media as a "charm offensive" that would also seek to check Bhutan-China relations that had recently been formalized. He also sought to build business ties, including a hydro-electric deal, and inaugurated the India-funded Supreme Court of Bhutan building, border management and service sector. While talking about the visit, Modi said that Bhutan was a "natural choice" for his first foreign destination because of the "unique and special relationship" the two countries shared. He added that he was looking forward to nurture and further strengthens India's special relations with Bhutan. His entourage included Foreign Minister Sushma Swaraj, National Security Adviser Ajit Doval and Foreign Secretary Sujatha Singh. During the visit he was also tried to discuss insurgency issue of North East. Till now he visited Bhutan 2 times as second time in the year of 2019.

If we discuss about the Narendra Modi's Bhutan Visit of 2014, important agreement were made between two countries;

- Reiterated their commitment to achieve 10,000 MW target in hydropower cooperation and no integration of territorial affairs of another.
- Measures and concession including the exemption of Bhutan from any ban on export of milk powder, wheat, edible oil, pulses and non basmati rice.
- Revolving the trade relation and expanding the bilateral relation in several arenas.
- Idea of relationship in the field of annual hill sport festival with Indian north eastern states along with Bhutan and Nepal.
- Modi announced increase in the scholarship being provided to Bhutanese student studying in India.

These two days Modi's trip was leading a new level development compares to the previous congress government. The Bhutanese king visited India in 2015 to attend Vibrant Gujarat Summit where several informal and formal discussions were hold between the countries. There has been several official level and informal level talks and discussion were held under the Modi's government. The trade between the two countries of 1972 Trade and Transit agreement was renewed in 2016; the agreement provides duty free transit of Bhutanese exports to third countries. As the member of the SAARC,

BIMSTEC both countries has a many talks and summit regarding regional issues and development. In 2015, India inks motor vehicle pact with Bhutan, Bangladesh, and Nepal with an aim to enable seamless transit of passenger and cargo vehicles among them. The Golden Jubilee of the establishment of formal diplomatic relation between two countries was being celebrated in the year 2018. The bilateral trade reached Rs/Nu. 9228 Cr. Imports from India were Rs/Nu. 6011 Cr. accounting for 84% of Bhutan's total imports Bhutan's exports to India stood at Rs/Nu. 3217 Cr. and Constituted 78% of its total exports. Some of the event or time line that were conducted under Narendra Modi government are mention below-

- Embassy between two countries organize a presentation on " Indian Budget (2015-16):Opportunities For Bhutan" on 6 march 2015
- 14th Meeting of Board of Directors of India-Bhutan Foundation at Thimpu ,11 March 2015
- India's ambassador interaction with Bhutanese media at India House, 27 march 2015
- Celebration of 2nd International Yoga Day at Thimpu, Bhutan 2016, 26 June
- Embassy of India organized A Business Event "Opportunities and Challenges in Doing Business with India" 22 March, 2016 at Taj Tashi, Thimpu.
- Mountain Echoes Summit between two Countries in 2016
- Visit of Nirmala Sitharaman Minister of State (Independent Charge) for commerce and Industry GoI to Bhutan,11-12 March 2016

- 5th India-Bhutan Annual Developmental Cooperation Talks took place on December 8, 2016
- The Golden Jubilee Commencement event of Laying down of Foundation stone of the India House , 4th May2018
- The First Indo-Bhutan feature film 'Singye' won four awards at 18th Bhutan National Film Awards organized on 21st February 2019.

In, 2019 Narendra visited Bhutan for the second time, between two counterparts there was talk on various developmental agenda, like

- RuPay card to be introduced in Bhutan for exchange of money and better digital development activities.
- In the Education field Interconnection between Indian National knowledge Network and DruKEN
- Ground station for the South Asian Satellite.
- Regarding the Hydroelectric Plant
- A stamp commemorating five decades of Indo-Bhutan Hydropower Cooperation.
- MoU between the Royal University of Bhutan and four leading Indian universities in Kanpur, Delhi, Silchar and Bombay.
- MoU between National Legal Institute of Bhutan and the National Judicial Academy of India.
- MoU between Department of Information Technology and Telecom, Ministry of Information and Communication and the Indian Space Research Organization.

These, are some time line and important agreement, talks, summit done under the Narendra Modi led BJP coalition government. During his tenure the relationship has been strengthening in a new rate and we are very much hopeful that in a upcoming year also the relationship between two countries stay cooperative in every occasion.

CHAPTER III

BODOLAND TERRITORIAL COUNCIL AND ITS ROLE

BTC Profile

Bodoland Territorial Council also known as Bodoland Territorial Area District (BTAD) was created in 2003 under the sixth schedule after signing a memorandum of settlement with Assam government, Indian Government and the Bodo Liberation Tigers.The agreement was covered to 3082 villages and has legislative powers over 40 subjects along with there are 40 Council elected constituencies and 6 members are nominated by the Governor of Assam. The Bodoland Territorial Council is headed by Hagrama Mohilary as Chief Executive Member and Deputy Chief as Kampa Borgoyari. The continuous struggle of Bodo community for its identity, social cultural and economic development got new meaning after signing this accord. The Jurisdiction of the agreement covers 25 developmental blocks, 13 revenue circles, 415 Village Council Development Committee. Towards this settlement there was a series of talks between Assam Government, Indian government and Bodoland Liberation Tigers from 2000, and it become reality in 2003. The objective of agreement was to create a Bodo community a more and autonomous power, within the state of Assam for the constitution safeguard of Bodo community in the field of educational, linguistic, infrastructure development and ethnic identity. The Bodoland Territorial Area comprise of Four District of Assam i.e. Kokrajhar, Chirang, Udalguri and Baksha located at the lower part of Assam. The area located by the Bodoland Territorial Council is gateway to all Northeast Indian states, if something bandh or close, violence happened to this area all the state are affected by it. Beside Bodo community, there are many communities like Rajbangsi, Adibasi, Garo, Muslim; Assamese are residing in the territorial region. In the region mostly people speak Bodo language and Assamese language. Since, Bodoland Territorial Area District is bounded by the Himalayan Kingdom of Bhutan in the North; the people of both countries are always busy to travel for various purposes which make them culturally strong. The people of Bodoland Territorial region has been a deep impact upon the developmental relation between two countries in social and cultural arena and to understand the role play by government of Bodoland Territorial Council and Its people become one of the most study topic.

Communities' role in developing a Friendly relation with Bhutan

Communities' role in developing a Friendly relation with Bhutan

There is very close relationship between communities of Bodoland region and people of Bhutan. People of Bhutan are locally known as Bhutanese and they are very kind and easy to make a friendship. In the bordering area people of both the countries has been living peacefully as brotherhood thought without any violence and prejudice. In the communication field, There is no language barriers between the people of both countries as Bhutanese people of bordering area also understand mixture of some language like Hindi, Bodo and Assamese, although in the area Bodo language has been mostly first priority vice versa people of Bodoland region also can speak fluent local dialect of Bhutan. Beside usual market every day, there is a weekly market on Friday, called Gelephu market in the Bordering area between two countries, here we can see lots local communities exchange their local products. This market gives a way peaceful and brotherhood relation to the people of this region. I have also experienced of going out there, as this weekly market is very famous in the Bodoland region, lots of people outside the Bodoland Territorial Council also come to explore this market or place. In the bordering area we can see several small stall own by local people as we can say that more than Five thousand families run their families by opening small business. Many people both from the Territorial region and outside territorial region as well as foreigner also come to visit nearby villages and market. Bhutanese people can easily enter India's territory without any governmental proof or ID card vice versa earlier Indian people also get easy entry to Bhutan, but after the February 2020, made a decision to ends free entry of Indian tourist but still local people also easily carried up their market activities regularly. This area play a important role in the in the transportation and communication field, as several goods carrying trucks, vehicle coming from West Bengal, Bihar and some from the North Eastern states enter through this Gelephu gate. This bordering region is very good steps for foreign policy of both the countries in the field of economy, tourism and as neighborhood first policy. As there has been demand from the Biswajit Dwimary, Member of Parliament from Assam from the Bodoland region local Bodoland Peoples Front party that this bordering area is very suitable for economic purposes and establishment of Rail link in this bordering area. Sometimes locals joins together to manage Border River as *The experience of managing the Saralbhanga River, which flows from Bhutan to India, shows the importance of peoples' participation for effective cooperation in Tran boundary Rivers.*There are as many as 56 rivers that flow down from the Himalayan kingdom of Bhutan to the eastern state of Assam in India to meet the Brahmaputra River. The hills of Bhutan are covered with lush forests, but on the Indian side of the border are vast tracts of dry plains with occasional patches of severely denuded forests.Downstream living communities in Assam have been regularly raising alarms about these developments, worried that the plans to build more dams in Bhutan will lead to increased flooding, erosion and more destruction than good. The Bhutanese government and their Indian dam consultants were dismissive about these objections in the past, but the rapid and extreme changes in weather patterns in the recent past has upset all predictions and is now shaping the future course of the river and Bhutan's relationship with India. At the community level, both men and women participate in all decision-making around the quantum of water to be lifted for each household and the contribution to the maintenance of the irrigation system. It is the women who have the most at stake and are the ones who want a more permanent solution, a treaty between the two countries if possible, so that there is better conversations on both sides of the border on flow of water.There is need to build on the foundation set by the students union and civil society on both sides of the border with continued strategic engagement to promote collective actions to mitigate and adapt to the climate change induced havoc playing out in these parts of western Assam. Peace is essential for implementation of any poverty alleviation and development programme in the region. Clearly, this successful interaction has led to increasing interest among local civil society organizations to participate in processes to influence practices at all levels in integrated water resource management that is more inclusive of community concerns. The idea of Rail linking is very good demand by the our led local Member of Parliament as it will boost countries economy along with local people will get huge advantage to this. The main point here, to understand is the development and cooperation between people of two countries, by combining people two countries it will lead to set a new foreign policy in field of Economy, Political, Security and Culturally. If we have to build perfect foreign policy it's also mandatory that people to people contact relation is very peaceful and there is no contradiction between the communities. It will be not wrong to say that people of this bordering area has been plying active role for determining developmental foreign policy.The golden anniversary of India-Bhutan Friendship offers a perfect opportunity for both the governments to explore how best to cooperate for joint projects to mitigate and adapt to the vagaries of our rivers in interest of citizens of both our countries. The King of Bhutan repeatedly expressed his interest in building on the past good relations with India to alleviate poverty and sufferings on both sides of the border and what better opportunity than to deal with this clear and present danger posed by this devastating consequence of climate change.

Relation with Bhutan before BTC

Before the Bodoland Territorial Council, it was known a Bodoland Autonomous Council, which was signed in 1993, the first accord of Bodo community with aim to socio economic development and identity safeguard but this accord failed to fulfill the aspiration of the Bodo community, then Second Bodo Accord came in the 2003. Before the BTC the Bodoland region was lacking behind in every purposes it may be education, economic, political and developmental policies. Communal violence, Riots and military activities were increasing during that time and making the developmental agenda fragile. There were no proper communication and transportation facility, as exchange of goods and services were carried out with the help of some animals like cow, horse, bull etc. Because, of lacking in infrastructural development the business opportunity was not good at that time and ups-down were very less. The Bodo communities were in to closer contact with the tribes of Bhutan by using local transportation facility. Commodities such as woolen blankets, yak's tail, Chinese silk, mules, musk-wax, rubber, goldust, rice,iron,cotton yarn and cloth, Assam silk yarn, buffalo horns, pearls, dries fish were sold in the market. There has been no problem in exchange of money also as people of both the countries as Indian people use Bhutanese Ngultrum currency and People of Bhutan use Indian currency. This kind of business activity and tradition has been continuing till now which make relation with Bhutan stronger. After, the end of 19 century there was an attempt from British East Indian Company to open overland route stretching from Northeast India in to far eastern side near Chinese border. During the late 20th century there were lots of trading market in the neighbouring border area but with the passage of time some trading location are changed in to another trading location. We can say that the Bhutias and people of Indian have thus a historical and cultural trade relation since long time. Starting from barter trade trade to trade with money, the business activities made by both countries significantly contribute to the growth of Bodo economy. The trade made by local people paved the way for many people who are coming from mainland India and try to settle in the bordering area. Further, it also witnessed the illegal outsiders come to Bodo inhabited border area and transfer of land from poor Bodo peasants to the outsiders. Despite, all this both the people of the countries shared their cultural traits through which their cordial bilateral border relation has further been strengthened.

Steps taken by Bodoland Territorial Council

After, the formation of Bodoland Territorial Council in Bodo dominated four districts, the socio economic developmental agenda was the main agenda that people of this region has been expecting. The BTC chief led by Hagrama Mohilary has been doing everything to develop the all the communities living in the Bodoland region but there also some negative side that BTC government has failed to reach the expectation of the local people. Before talking about political environment of the Bodoland region, let's discuss about the steps and action taken by the BTC government. BTC government has been taking efficient steps to take develop friendly cooperation with neighbouring Bhutan starting from infrastructure to insurgency from in entire North East India. It would be not wrong to say that BTC government has equal cooperation and understanding with Bhutanese official like what the relation has between the Bhutanese government and Indian government.

Communication and Transportation

Starting from infrastructure, earlier the road was not suitable for the running of vehicle and business activities, afterwards BTC government took quite good step in order to improve transportation facility. In present condition we can see the increasing ups and down between two sides.

In Bodoland region, there some road or highway, by which we can enter Bhutan one is through the Chirang district via Samtaibari road, mostly used highway by the people and other road such as Saralpara in Kokrajhar district, Simla, Bwirabkunda which are mostly use by local people in direct to direct contact. Some of the great steps taken by BTC government with the help of Assam government are-

In 2016, there was press release from the Assam government that in order start Indo-Bhutan international highway, talks has been going on with the union ministry of highways, road transport and shipping to draw a roadmap for connecting India with Bhutan by constructing an international highway via Assam's Bodoland Territorial Area District region.
Chief minister Sarbananda Sonowal said that the proposed highway would prove vital in improving trade, cultural exchange, cooperation and commerce between the two nations.
Rounds of talks have been hold between the state government officials and the centre for strengthening road connectivity with the neighbouring country, for the proper development Bodoland Territorial Region, which Assam shares long border. He also, said this while laying the foundation stone for a RCC Bridge over Bharola River on Tamulpur-Udalguri Road under Udalguri assembly constituency.
The bridge was a part of road project "Improvement and up-gradation of Road section of Tamulpur to Paneri and Paneri to Udalguri in Assam under North Eastern States

Road Investment Project (NESRIP).

The chief minister also laid the foundation stone of Suklai River Bridge and Kala-Nanoi River Bridge under Paneri assembly constituency on Tamulpur-Paneri Road and Bornadi River Bridge under Tamulpur assembly constituency as part of the NESRIP Trance-II Project.

On the sidelines of the foundation stone laying ceremony at Suklai and Kala-Nanoi River Bridge, Chief Minister Sonowal also visited the Barangajuli Srimanta Sankardev Satra and interacted with the Satradhikar.

Sonowal said that Prime Minister Narendra Modi has laid utmost priority in improving surface communication in Assam for ushering development in northeastern region. This International highway will be huge boost to Bodo dominated area for business related activities and other developmental activities.

State Social Welfare and Soil Conservation Minister **Pramila Rani Brahma who is Local MLA from Bodoland Peoples Front** laid the foundation stones of the model village roads and India Gate at Saralpara along the Indo-Bhutan border in Kokrajhar district. Both these schemes was planning to implement at the cost of Rs. 8.52 crore and Rs. 2.22 crore under **Border Area Development programme** for the year 2017-18 and 2018-19 respectively.During the programme, the minister said that taking initiative for transforming Saralpara into a model village was her first choice as the people of the area were facing many problems regarding potable drinking water, higher education, healthcare facilities and housing. According to her, implementation of this project will become easier to construct health centre's, roads, school buildings, and a playground, supply electricity, creates drinking water facilities, tourist spots and builds toilets. It will help in implementing various development schemes of the government in this village. Brahma hoped that the India Gate which would be constructed near the Indo-Bhutan border at Naharani, Saralpara would be able to attract tourists and help in regulating trade between both countries. The programme was attended by Bhaskar Das, Additional Deputy Commissioner, Jagamahan Basumatary, Additional Chief Engineer and Council Head of Department, PWD, BTC, Rajesh Kr. Singh, Assistant Commandant, SSB, Saralpara and other dignitaries. Saralpara area is very close contact with the neighbouring Bhutan and its place of picnic spot also, after the successful completion of this project I believe that there will be enough development to improve the livelihood of this areas people.

These are some of the important action or policies taken by BTC government in collaboration with Assam Government and Government of India in the field of Transportation and communication which will help people of both the countries in crating brotherhood relationship.

Socio-Cultural-Linguistic

Socio-Cultural relationship is the main power point behind the increasing relationship and cooperation with Bhutanese people in the bordering area. The exchange of culture and Social customs held every day in the bordering area from the commodities buying and selling activities. Beside, this the BTC government also taking effective measures to use Socio-Cultural means as a weapons of developing relationships. Some of the important programs and policies regarding Socio-Cultural field are mention below-

In the month of January, 2020 The 10th Indo-Bhutan Friendship Fair and 68th Subankhata Maghw Mela has organized by BTC administration with a eight day long programme at Subankhata along the India-Bhutan border border in Assam's Baksa district .Hundreds of visitors from both India and Bhutan gathered in the program . This fair is organized every year during third week of January to celebrate the bond between the two friendly countries and showcases the culture and traditions of both the countries. The Indo-Bhutan friendship fair is being organized to boost bilateral relations between India and Bhutan as a part of confidence building measures at Subankhata along the Indo-Bhutan border in Assam's Baksa district for the past ten years. The citizens of greater Subankhata area, situated in the northern part along the Bhutan border in Baksa district of Assam has been organizing Maghw Fair since six decades where citizens from both India and Bhutan come to the fair every year and have a feel of peace and unity among society in the region.The Bhutanese merchants from Pemagatshel and Samdrup Jongkhar sell mandarin, ginger, soyabean, and potatoes etc during the fair. Earlier, Bhutanese merchants used to camp at Subankhata for

months and witness the fair and recount the fun and wonders they experienced with their friends and family back home and tradition of Bhutanese going down to Subankhata continued well until 1990s.
With passage of time the age-old Magh fair continued to be organized on the other side of the border. The Bhutanese people were encouraged to put up stalls to showcase Bhutanese tradition and cultural programmes and thus Maghw renamed as Indo-Bhutan Friendship Fair. During the fair the cuisine and culture, which are the best ways to foster relationship, pays an important part in the Indo-Bhutan mela.Bodoland Territorial Council executive member Bijit Gwra Narzary inaugurated the main gate of the fair amidst huge crowd on the inaugural day.Stalls serving both Bhutanese Bodo and Assamese cuisine were set up to the huge crowd. Traditional dances during the fair provided a window to the culture and traditions of both the countries. General Secretary of Bhutan India Friendship Association Norbu Wangdi said that the fair has been able to bring cooperation and understanding between both the countries which is increasing with every year and this maghw fair is paving the way for boosting economic activities amongst both the countries.Member of Bodoland Territorial Council (MCLA) and chief patron of the fair committee Phalindra Basumatary said that that the fair is being organized every year to foster a deep relation and cooperation between India and Bhutan.

In order to make tourism sector higher and attract more tourist from neighbouring Bhutan and Nepal,

Bhairabkunda Tourism festival is organized by BTC government every year. Bhairabkunda -a picturesque tri-junction located in the Bodoland Territorial Region of Assam, Arunachal Pradesh and Bhutan and to register its unmatched natural beauty on the tourism map of the country, the seventh edition of Bhairabkunda festival was organized with at Bhairabkunda.
A reception-cum-festival management committee to this effect was formed with State Minister Rihon Daimari, Speaker of BTC Assembly, Tridip Daimari, and MCLA of Bhairabkunda BTC constituency, Ripen Daimari as president, working president and secretary respectively.The celebration committee members said that the Bhairabkunda festival would reflect the age-old bond of fraternity, unity and integrity among the diverse ethnic linguistic groups, including those from neighbouring Bhutan and Arunachal Pradesh, and its mission was to give an exposure to the tourism prospects, self-employment opportunities for the educated unemployed youths and to promote communal harmony and tranquility in the region.
The festival was also feature cultural exchange programmes among Bhutan, Arunachal Pradesh and Assam.

To improve socio cultural and business sector, a decision was made to export Indian handicrafts from Assam's Bodoland Territorial Council to Bhutan, a Memorandum of Understanding (MoU) was signed with Bhutan Chambers of Commerce and Industry (BCCI).The MoU was signed by Rana Patgiri, Managing Director, Bodoland

Regional Apex Weavers & Artisans Cooperative Federation Ltd (BRAWFED) and Chandra B Chhetri, Deputy Secretary General, BCCI in presence of the Chairman, BRAWFED. Both side resolved to organize the 7th Thematic Exhibition on Indian Handicraftsalong with the Bhutan-India Trade & Investment Promotion Expo and the 4th Agri-Flori Fair 2018 in commemoration of the Golden Jubilee of Formal Diplomatic Relations between Bhutan-India 1968-2018 under separate pavilions.It was held from September 12 to September 16, 2018 at the Changlimithang National Stadium Parking Ground, Thimphu.The 7th Thematic ExhibitionIndian Handicraft had 40 standard stalls with a platform for live demonstration by master craftsperson from the BTC and space for thematic display of Indian handicrafts. BRAWFED hold 'Border to Border' meeting during the 7th TEIH as a market promotional program and BCCI invited local buyers/stakeholders from Thimphu for business purposes as well as a means of social cultural exchange. The marketing of the 7th TEIH among potential Indian participants was undertaken entirely by the BRAWFED.

The sports and games competition between two countries also contributing lots in developing relation. In the Bodoland region when any football and sports completion is conducted People from came to participate in. An Indo-Bhutan women's friendly football match was conducted by the Bodoland Territorial Sports ministry with Bhutan sports department as a international friendly match. The friendly tourney was organized at Banargaon rural mini stadium here between Sports Authority of India (SAI), and Bhutan Women's Football Club, Gelephu.The friendly women's football match was organized to create bondage between India and Bhutan.These are the some of the important steps taken by BTC administration in the field of Socio cultural linguistic cooperation and development of foreign policy relation.

Trade Relation

In the field of Market and trade BTC government has gradually taking effective measures.There are many border markets on the plains of Assam, adjoining to the Bhutan hills as those market areas has been becoming attractive tourist place. Of all these markets, Udalguri market was considerably the biggest one, where the Bhutia mela continued to be held annually. This occurred, often because of the existence of a famous border trade route so called Lhasa (Tibet) - Tawang-Udalguri route of 5000 rupees to the Bhutia chiefs as a guarantee for maintaining safety and peace all along the route up to Tawang. As a result, the Udalguri-Tawang-Lhasa trade route again opened and thereafter an annual Bhutia melabazar held at Udalguri, and continued till recent past. There is, of course, a reference of annual posa paid continuously to the Bhutia representatives in 1944 CE. Trade relations between India and Bhutan got a big push by the opening of a border trade centre by Assam chief minister Sarbananda Sonowal in the town of Baksadistrict. An industries and commerce department official said Indian investment in Bhutan is the highest among all nations and there is still huge scope to give it impetus.

The border trade centre is a right initiative in that respect, the official said. The Central government had released Rs 14 crore for the centre and work completed last year.Darranga is adjacent to Samdrup Jongkhar in East Bhutan. India exports essential items like food materials, LPG, kerosene, petroleum products, including machinery and accessories, meat and fish to Bhutan while it imports potato, gypsum, Ferro-silicon and oranges.

However, stagnation in business exchange especially at places adjoining east Bhutan border near Rangiya, Nagrijuli, Tamulpur etc; have kept the small businessmen here worried. After signing of the first ever friendship treaty in 1865 between India and Bhutan, relations with Assam had been very conducive. With the eastern part of Bhutan lying very close to Rangiya subdivision in Kamrup district, people had been familiar with the neighbouring country's people, customs, and benefited from the country's trade business. It was through Darranga mela here, that essential commodities including rice, oranges, woolen garments etc; were traded. After temporary halt in business. East Bhutan has now opted for West Bengal for procuring various raw and finished products for its use. Bhutan businessmen have opted for other places for exchange of vital items like dal, clothes and machineries, etc; from Indian market. Also, many of the local businessmen are concerned here that Rangiya has lost out on trade items like gypsum material from Bhutan, coal, and other at valuable forest goods the exchange of which between Bhutan and to India is going on regularly. Opting distant places for procuring for essential goods from India by Bhutanese people has affected the economic development of this place. As, there was a strong business relationship albeit on a small scale in the border areas, people of Rangiya, Tamulpur, Nagrijuli etc; Samrupjonghar, Darranga near Bhutan, and at other bordering areas were greatly benefited. Based on the 16th SAARC summit at Thimphu, Royal Bhutan Government and the Government of India should consider strengthening the relations between both the countries and give ample scope of earning of livelihood to the people of both the countries by restoring the business hubs at places like Darrranga mela. The transport and communication facility has been improved after the coming of BTC government.

BTC government and peace and security and Effect on Bhutan Foreign Policy

Here, the point to study is about some military organization and their role in the Bodoland Territorial Region which affected a lot in the economy and security of both the countries. BTC chief Hagrama Mohilary has been raising the issue of NDFB (Disband), KLO, ULFA since the long time. Beside this military organization many other small faction of group has been active in breaking the security rules and crating a tension in the bordering area. So, in this case BTC government has been pressuring both the State government and Central government in solving the military problem in the region. Bhutan has been suffering a lot of military problem also which are mostly Indian based military organization, in this case if something operation happened against the military organization, they also become victims. Bhutan had faced enough experience of bitterness in the decade-long insurgency problems in Assam and Bodoland Territorial Council (BTC) region as it suffered lot of problems while entering India.There are a lot of sad stories of attack and counter attack between the insurgent group and Government forces in the region and every time Bhutan foreign policy has been affected by it. There have been a number of military operations against insurgency group who are active in Northeast region or with specially NDFB (Disband) who had been mostly active in Bodoland area in the foothills of Bhutan.

In 1990 India Army launched Operations Rhino and Bajrang against Assam separatist groups. Facing continuous pressure, Assamese militants relocated their camps to Bhutan.In the 1990s, United Liberation Front of Assam (ULFA) and National Democratic Front of Bodoland (NDFB) allegedly assisted the government of Bhutan in the expulsion of the ethnic Lhotshampa population, occupying the land left behind by the refugees.In 1996 the Bhutan government became aware of a large number of camps on its southern border with India. The camps were set up by four Assamese separatist movements: the ULFA, NDFB, Bodo Liberation Tigers Force (BLTF) and Kamtapur Liberation Organization (KLO). The camps also harbored separatists belonging to the National Socialist Council of Nagaland (NSCN) and All Tripura Tiger Force (ATTF).The camps had been established with the goal of training cadres and storing equipment, while the thick jungles of the region also enabled the militants to easily launch attacks into Indian Territory.India then exerted diplomatic pressure on Bhutan, offering support in removing the rebel organizations from its soil. The government of Bhutan initially pursued a peaceful solution, opening dialogue with the militant groups on 1998.

Operation such as Operation All clear which was conducted by Royal Bhutan Army forces against Assam separatist insurgent group in the southern region of

Bhutan between the years of 2003-2004. In 2014, Indian Army launched Operation All Out against NDFB(S) now disband. Along with cooperation of armies of Bhutan and Myanmar in order to prevails peace in the region. During the lunched of operation all out Bhutanese P.M Tshering Tobgay has assured its support to India in its action against the insurgency group. In order to solve the insurgency problem the Chief of BTC has been taking active role as he discussed with the Central government and State government regarding the insurgency issues in the North East region. So this kind of stories has been affecting the developmental relation between India and Bhutan, which need to be given utmost importance.

In the Month of January/2020the general secretary of Bhutan-India Friendship Association (BIFA), Gelegphu Chapter Ugen Rabten in a conversation said that he noticed series of positive developments in Assam after the new line of signing new accord with the factions of National Democratic Front of Bodoland (NDFB) as soon as possible. He said that the steps taken by the Government of India was praiseworthy and permanent peace will prevail in the plains of Assam and BTC region as well.Rabten said, "Well, with such positive developments in the neighborhood, we are more than happy and I personally extend my appreciation to the government of India and, of course, for the hard work of BTC Chief Hagrama Mohilary." He said after several decades of unrest and bloodshed for the cause of Bodoland, now they will begin to see a streak of silver line to accomplish the hopes and aspirations of Bodoland people. This peaceful way of negotiating the talks between the stakeholders will not only foster positive resolution but will bring respite to them in the Himalayas because they being the closest neighbor are almost every day moving in and out through the long stretch of highways that run through BTC, he said.The BIFA general secretary hopes that the sacrifices of the people of Bodoland and the initiatives of the Government of India and BTC will bear the fruits of success and jointly usher in a new era of progress and happiness for Bodoland which certainly is going to have regional peace and harmony for all neighborhoods.BTC administration has been discussing this insurgency problem of North East India since many years both at the national and central level to come up in a fruitful solution.

BTC Government and Bhutan Way Forward

Beside Indian government, BTC administration and Bhutan also share time tested relationship. For, the development of BTC region there is needed to take some steps again in the field of economy, culture, insurgency etc. For, India to augment and maintain this indispensable relationship may not be difficult, provided India assists to make Bhutan self reliant militarily, politically and economically. BTC administration has a big role to play also as a factor of bordering region and maintenance of insurgency group, information about the strategic and security information to Central government. Indian policy makers must keep in mind that Bhutan is an independent nation and not India's pawn. Thus the relationship must be characterized by quid quo and not for only the benefit of India. Indian can give ideas and strides to make Bhutan economically competitive and self reliant in the matters of national security to gain the trust of the Bhutanese population. Aspiration of the Bhutanese population must be considered before making any economic and political decision about Bhutan. Steps must be taken to maintain this long standing relationship by not interfering in domestic politics and the economic decision of Bhutan, if this is not done there is a possibility that China may take advantage of this situation and India may not have the control it currently enjoys in Bhutan. In the people to people and community socio cultural exchange programs BTC government can take active role in upcoming days as this will lead to a strong cultural bonding and change in the foreign policy. Steps can be taken in collaboration with BTC government, Assam government and Central government in the Tourism sector as place in the bordering region is very attractive for visitors and in the present scenario the tourist place are not developed as expectation. People of both countries must understand that rules and regulation must be followed and no violation of socio-cultural rules of another country as we have seen in recent days that after travelling to Bhutan, violation of Bhutan Religious spirits. We must have to understand that the policy of neighborhood and Bhutan as the major country in the neighbor to determines the developmental foreign policy.

From, BTC administration it must be sure that fund must be succefully allocated to development of infrastructure, bridges and organize social cultural activities, several schemes will be deployed in relation to Bhutan administration for the successful development of both the countries. BTC administration must conscious about the matter that many indigenous people living in the bordering area spend their lives in engaging tertiary activities and can do lot more in the bordering region in the field of infrastructure, market place, some effective developmental policy towards the bordering region.Being, neighbors it is necessary that both nations continuously recognize value of each other. For, these regular high level visits from both sides are important. Safety of border from China is a concern for both nations. Therefore, both sides need to work together on this issue. Also, it needs to be ensured that borders areas remains militants free. Therefore, Bhutan plays a significant role in India's foreign policy and only neighbouring country that is not under the influence of China, making it strategically and location ally important for both the countries. If steps are not taken to improve Bhutan, it might be exploited by China; to strengthen its already dominant position in South Asia and might lost the important value of developmental agenda in the region. So, I hope that in upcoming days BTC government in collaboration with State government and Central government take best to best policy in the benefits and development of both the countries.

CHAPTER IV

CONCLUSION

Summary of Findings

This chapter reviews the key findings of the present research and certain policy measures. As the objective of the study is understand developing relationship between India and Bhutan, the study give us understanding that relation has been growing in a faster rate in the 21st century compared to 20th century. The plan and policies of the Indian government clarifies that neighborhood countries plays a important role in the countries developing position in the international level vice versa that's why it is must that we have give importance to neighbouring countries. The foreign policy of India has been changing towards Bhutan and Bhutan also affecting India's foreign policy structure. Either it may be Congress or BJP government, they are giving equal importance to Bhutan and taking Bhutan as friendship to counter Chinas dominance in the region.

Bibliography:-

Acharya, NN: “A Brief History of Assam” Omsous Publications, New Delhi (2007).

Barpujari, HK: “North East India: Politics and Prospects since independence”. Spectrum Publications, Guwahati-781001, 1998.

Basumatary, Ionee: “Politics in North East India” BishalPrakashan, Guwahati-781003 (2014).

Baruah, Sanjib: “India Against Itself, Assam and the politics of Nationality”. Oxford University Press, New Delhi-110001, 1999.

Chaudhuri, Kalyan: “New History of Assam and India” Oriental Book Company Private LTD, Guwahati (2004).

Printed by Libri Plureos GmbH in Hamburg,
Germany